EARLY DINOSAURS

Have an adult help you remove the stickers.

Phidal

Did You Know?

Dinosaurs lived during three periods called the Triassic, the Jurassic, and the Cretaceous. Find out more about the earliest dinosaurs with your stickers.

During the Triassic Period, the Earth's continents were one supercontinent called Pangaea.

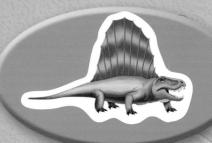

Animals like lizards and amphibians existed before the earliest dinosaurs.

When dinosaurs first walked the Earth, it was warm and dry.

Dinosaurs hatched from eggs the way reptiles and birds do today.

Many bones of early dinosaur skeletons are missing because they are very old and fragile.

Many of the earliest dinosaurs were meat-eaters that walked on two legs.

The first dinosaurs were really small; it wasn't until the Jurassic Period that dinosaurs became much larger.

The Eoraptor was three feet long, about the size of a fox.

Dinosaurs are categorized by their hip bones. The two kinds are lizard-hipped and bird-hipped.

Plateosaurus was one of the largest early dinosaurs. It measured over 26 feet long—the size of a freight truck!

Herrerasaurus lived in South America and is one of the oldest meat-eating dinosaurs ever found.

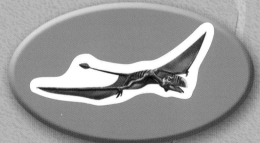

Pterosaurs were flying reptiles that first lived during the Triassic Period.

Triassic Dinosaur Facts

The first dinosaurs of the Triassic Period appeared after an earlier mass extinction that wiped out most life on Earth. Discover some more exciting dinosaur details below!

Melanorosaurus is one of the earliest sauropods, or long-necked dinosaurs, who walked on all fours.

The long neck of the Plateosaurus allowed it to reach leaves and branches high off the ground.

Pisanosaurus is an early Triassic dinosaur known only by one partial skeleton found in Argentina.

Coleophysis was a pack animal, which means that it preferred traveling with several of its own kind.

Liliensternus, a close relative of Coleophysis, had prominent crests on its head.

Eocursor was a speedy, small, long-beaked dinosaur with a mouth full of sharp, triangular teeth.

The jawbones of the earliest known dinosaurs belonged to plant-eaters like the Sellosaurus.

The Scutellosaurus had sharp front teeth to grab plants, while the teeth on the side of its jaws had tiny ridges that helped slice its food.

Herrerasaurus' skeleton was incomplete for 30 years before a paleontologist finally found its skull.

Staurikosaurus remains are rare because it may have lived in a forest environment where bones didn't fossilize.

The Shonisaurus was a dolphin-like fish from the Ichthyosaur family that measured over 50 feet long.

A major extinction occurred at the end of the Triassic Era, but dinosaurs survived and went on to dominate the Jurassic.

Triassic Transformation

With the shifting of the supercontinents at the end of the Triassic Era, many creatures were wiped out from climate change. Dinosaurs lived on! Decorate the scene below.

Dinosaur Identification

The first dinosaurs were smaller versions of the later giants that dominated the Earth. Use your stickers to get a better look at these early species.

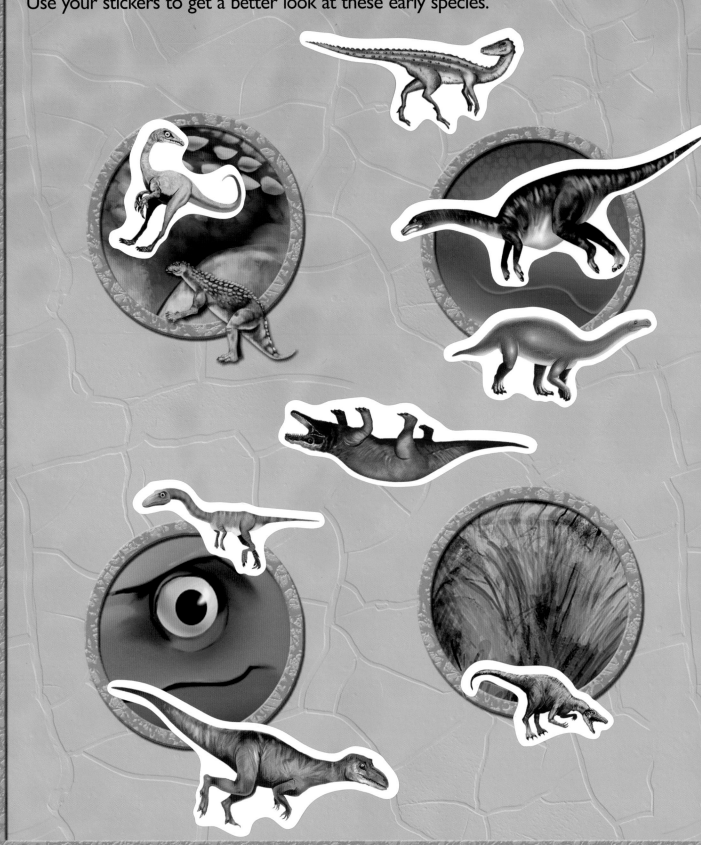

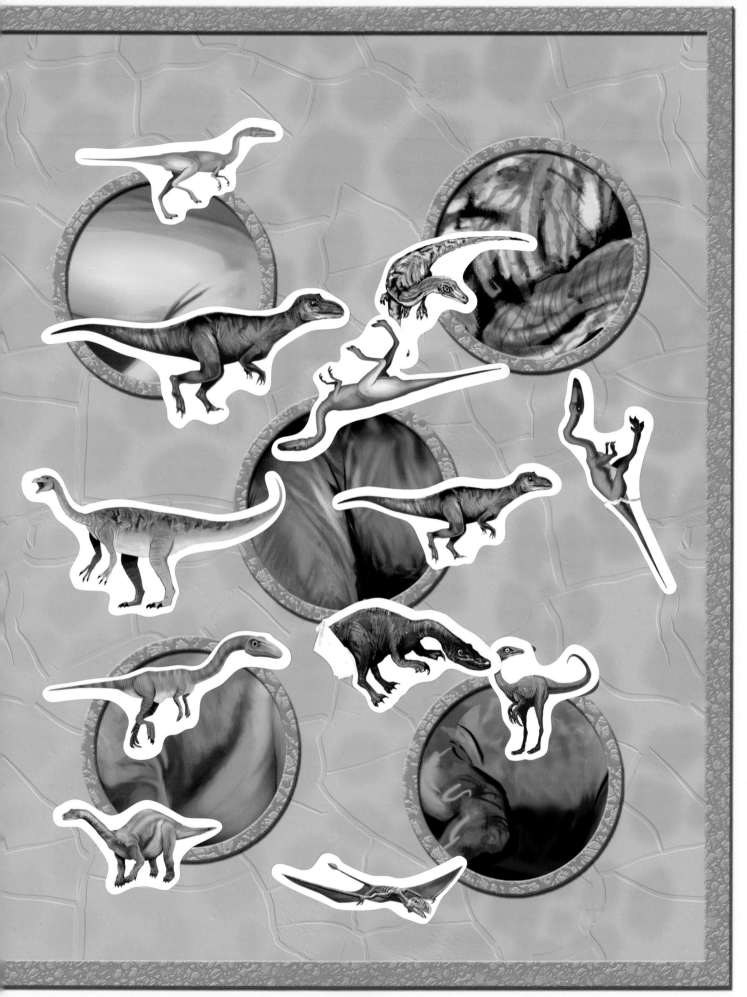

Which Dinosaur...

There are so many different types of dinosaurs! Who was fast, and who was slow? With the help of your stickers, place each dinosaur over the right shadow below.

...is super speedy?

...walks on all fours?

...has a crest on its head?

...is brown?

...swims in the water?

Prehistoric Plant Life

The early to mid-Triassic Period saw a burst of new life and the spread of different plants and ferns. Decorate this green scene with your stickers.

Can You Spot?

Discover the names of these early dinosaurs with the help of your stickers.

Sellosaurus

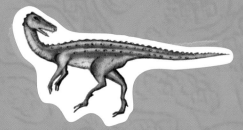

Scutellosaurus

Pisanosaurus

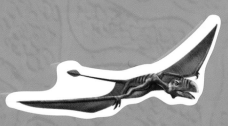

Pterosaur

Eoraptor

JURASSIC GIANTS

Have an adult help you remove the stickers.

Did You Know?

The Jurassic Era is considered to be the golden age of dinosaurs. Place your stickers with the right facts below to learn more about these amazing creatures.

The Megalosaurus was a gigantic meat-eater and the first dinosaur to be scientifically named in 1824.

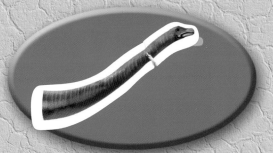

The Mamenchisaurus is the dinosaur with the longest neck at 36 feet long, about half of its total length.

The Tuojiangosaurus had spikes on its shoulders for extra protection.

The name Stegosaurus means "roof reptile" because it was first thought that its back plates lay flat like the tiles on a roof.

The Diplodocus was a plant-eating dinosaur that had the longest tail.

The femur or the upper leg bone of an Apatosaurus was about six feet long—way taller than the average person!

While the Dilophosaurus was first discovered in 1942, its remains were difficult to study and it wasn't officially named until 1970.

The Seismosaurus, whose name means "earth shaker," was the longest land animal to have ever lived at over 130 feet long!

If you stood beside the leg of a Brachiosaurus you would barely reach past the dinosaur's knee bone!

Brachiosaurus had large nostrils on the top of its head which suggests that it might have had a very keen sense of smell.

Compsognathus was one of the smallest dinosaurs ever discovered—its size was similar to that of a young rooster!

Allosaurus and its relatives were the largest predators of the Jurassic world.

Jurassic Dinosaur Facts

During the Jurassic Period, dinosaurs and reptiles continued to evolve, and the first known birds appeared. Discover more impressive facts below.

Massospondylus' food was probably mashed in its stomach because its small teeth weren't strong enough to chew much plant food.

Archaeopteryx is an early-known bird that evolved during the Jurassic to share the skies with flying reptiles called pterosaurs.

The Dilophosaurus was a terrifying meat-eater that used its opposable thumbs to grasp its prey.

Jurassic dinosaurs were much larger than the first dinosaurs of the earlier Triassic Period.

The supercontinent Pangaea began to split apart during the Jurassic and landmasses started to look more like the shapes they are today.

Pterosaur bones were hollow, which made them lightweight and delicate but more difficult to fossilize.

Plesiosaurs were marine
reptiles with long necks like the
one pictured here.

Ichthyosaurs were fish-like
reptiles that swam in the waters
during the Jurassic.

The Rhamphorhynchus was a long-tailed
pterosaur whose tail-tip ended in a web that
was shaped like a diamond.

Compared to other pterosaurs,
Anurognathus had a short tail, which made
it easier to maneuver during a hunt.

Scientific evidence suggests that Sordes Pilosus,
which was about the size of a pigeon, did not
have a head crest like most pterosaurs.

Metriorhynchus was an ancient marine
crocodile that, unlike today's version, had less
armor in order to swim faster.

Traveling Titans

Dinosaurs grew to epic sizes and spread out in huge numbers during the Jurassic Period. Create your own prehistoric scene below.

Small-Scales & Great Giants

While some dinosaurs were as small as today's pigeons, several dinosaurs grew to gigantic proportions. Use your stickers to see some of them below.

Herbivore Hang-Out

The Jurassic climate was lush with vegetation, ideal for the plant-eaters of the time. With the help of your stickers, make the scene below look like the one above.

Prehistoric Patterns

Just as in nature today, there were predators and prey among dinosaurs in the prehistoric world. Match each dinosaur with the right pattern.

Can You Spot?

Find out the names of these Jurassic giants with the help of your stickers.

Compsognathus

Ichthyosaur

Archaeopteryx

Stegosaurus

Sordes Pilosus

DINOSAURS

THE LAST DINOSAURS

Have an adult help you remove the stickers.

Phidal

Cretaceous Creatures

The Cretaceous Period lasted from 145 to 65 million years ago, and was the last era of dinosaurs. Place your stickers over the shadows to learn more!

Tyrannosaurus rex's name comes from the Greek phrase meaning "Tyrant King of the Lizards."

Some of the last species to evolve during the Cretaceous Period were the horned ceratopsians.

The Parasaurolophus had a long crest on its head that contained two hollow tubes which allowed it to make sounds.

Pteranodon was a flying carnivore… but it had no teeth! It often swallowed its food whole.

Snakes made their first appearance during the Cretaceous Period. They were the first legless lizards.

Few tracks show the marks of a tail, which suggests that dinosaurs did not drag their tails, they held them above the ground.

Of all the known dinosaurs, Pentaceratops had the largest head. Its skull was over nine feet long!

Hadrosaurus' beak-shaped snout had no teeth; however, it had many plant-grinding teeth deep in its jaws.

It was in Cretaceous times that the continents were broken up and distinct landmasses were created.

Triceratops had a short horn above its mouth and two long horns above its eyes to defend itself from predators.

Although the Tyrannosaurus' arms were relatively small, they were powerful enough to lift over 450 pounds.

Hesperonychus was a very small dinosaur. It is estimated to have weighed about four to five pounds… that's less than a housecat!

Discovering Dinosaurs

Some of the most memorable dinosaur species lived through the Cretaceous Period, including T. rex and Triceratops! Use your stickers to discover more interesting facts.

Sauroposeidon was the dinosaur with the longest neck. Some of its individual neck bones are up to four feet long!

Therizinosaurus had the longest claws of any animal that's ever lived. They were about two feet long!

Majungatholus bones have been found with tooth marks of other Majungatholus, which suggests that this dinosaur preyed on its own kind.

Although land turtles had already existed for millions of years, the first sea turtles appeared during the Cretaceous Era.

The Bambiraptor was discovered by a 14-year-old boy who was hunting for fossils near Montana's Glacier National Park.

Giganotosaurus is the largest predatory dinosaur found to date. It weighed eight tons… that's two tons more than T. rex!

T. rex was a very agile dinosaur.
Evidence suggests that it could run
10 to 25 miles per hour.

The Corythosaurus had a
duck-like bill that made it easier
to scoop food up off the ground.

The Spinosaurus' crocodile-like
snout helped it hunt for fish
in deep water.

Pachycephalosaurus means
"thick-headed dinosaur."

Fossils show that Baryonyx
possessed a set of very sharp,
hook-like teeth.

Deinonychus had a flexible tail.
It would swish from side to side to
counter-balance its weight.

A Trip to the Swamp

The swamp was a great place for Cretaceous dinosaurs to swim and eat. Decorate the scene to discover what these dinosaurs are up to!

Fascinating Footprints

Footprints can tell us how fast a dinosaur ran, and whether it walked on two legs or four. Match these dinosaurs to their tracks.

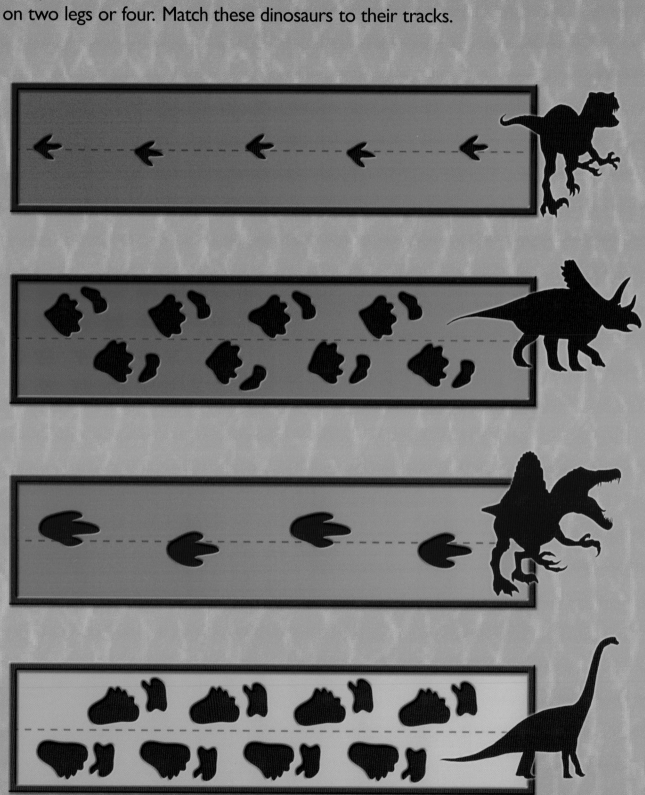

Dinosaur Close-Ups

It's time to get up close and personal with some Cretaceous creatures!
Match your dinosaur stickers to the right close-ups.

Creature Categories

There were many different types of dinosaurs that roamed the Earth during the Cretaceous Period. Place each dinosaur in the category to which it belongs.

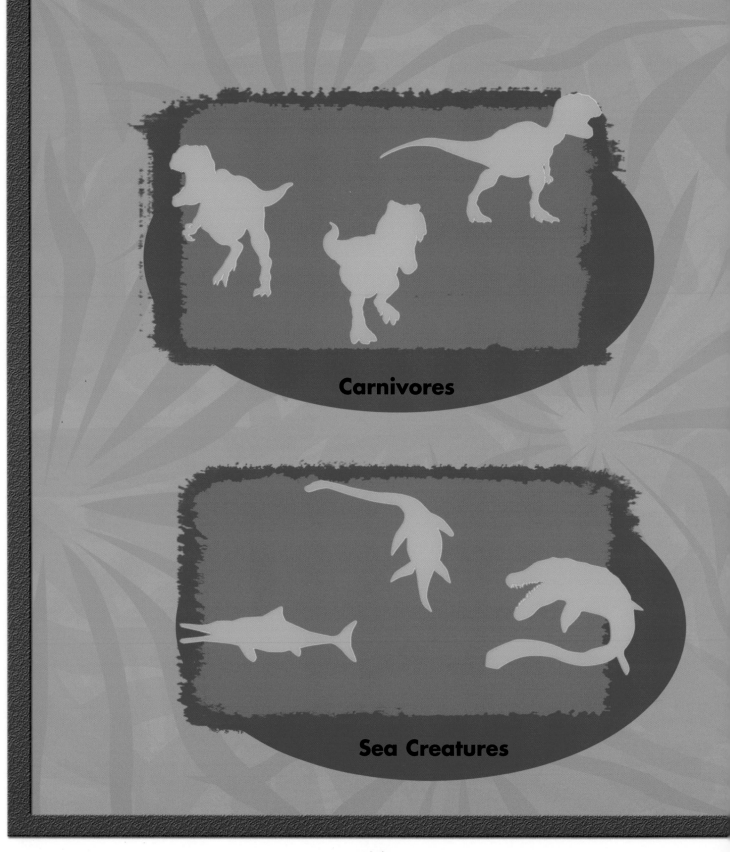

Carnivores

Sea Creatures

Herbivores

Flying Creatures

Can You Spot?

These dinosaurs walked the Earth long before humans existed! Complete the scene by placing your stickers over the right shadows.

Tyrannosaurus rex

Pentaceratops

Pachycephalosaurus

Parasaurolophus

Majungatholus

BONES AND FOSSILS

Have an adult help you remove the stickers.

Phidal

Fossil Facts

No one knows exactly what caused the extinction of dinosaurs. Popular theories suggest that it may have been an asteroid, climate change, or extreme volcanic activity.

Dinosaur fossils were created when wet mud dried around a dinosaur's body.

People who excavate small fossils work with very fine tools to make sure not to damage them.

Scientists who study fossils are called paleontologists.

Scientists use fossils to help put together dinosaur skeletons.

Fossilized teeth help scientists determine whether a dinosaur ate plants, meat, or both.

The oldest fossilized dinosaur egg discovered in North America is about 150 million years old!

The largest dinosaur skeletons
belong to long-necked herbivores
called sauropods.

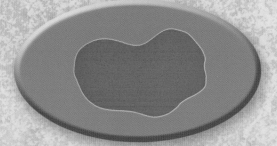

A fossilized footprint can indicate
whether a dinosaur walked
on two legs or four.

Some amber fossils, made from hardened
tree sap, have perfectly preserved insects
that lived alongside the dinosaurs.

Recent fossil discoveries suggest
that some dinosaurs may
have had feathers.

A dinosaur's fossilized stomach
contents can tell scientists
what it liked to eat.

The position of the dinosaur bones
can help scientists understand
how the creature died.

Fun with Fossils

Although dinosaurs have been extinct for millions of years, the discovery of their fossilized bones can tell us a lot about their lives! Discover some amazing facts below.

Researchers use a geologic map to look for layers of rock that are the same age as the fossils they want to find.

Fossilized dinosaur footprints can be as small as just a few inches across, or as large as a few feet across!

Vertebrate fossils are fossils of animals with bones.

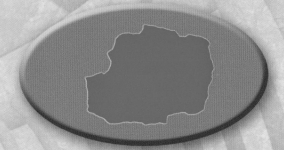

Invertebrate fossils are fossils of plants and animals that didn't have bones.

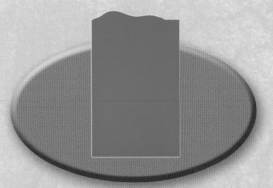

Stratigraphy is a dating method that estimates a fossil's age based on how deeply it is buried in the ground.

The size and spacing of tooth marks found on fossilized bones help scientists determine which dinosaur attacked it!

The most complete T. rex fossil ever discovered is 13 feet high and 42 feet long, and is nicknamed "Sue"!

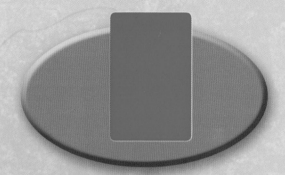

X-rays can help scientists see parts of a fossil that might otherwise be hidden.

In 2001, a 110 million-year-old "SuperCroc" fossil was discovered. The 40-foot-long creature weighed 17,500 pounds!

Paleontologists sometimes use acid to erode the rocks around a fossil without damaging the fossil itself.

Thanks to fossils, scientists now recognize over 330 different dinosaur species!

The jaw and teeth of the Megalosaurus were the first dinosaur fossils discovered in England in 1824.

At the Museum

Fossils allow scientists to create replicas of dinosaur bones, which can be displayed for everyone to enjoy. Decorate the exhibit with your stickers.

Digging for Dinosaurs

Now it's your turn to be a paleontologist! Using your stickers, assemble the fossilized dinosaur at the museum.

Prehistoric Fossils

Although dinosaurs are no longer around, their shapes are sometimes found preserved in fossils. Can you match each creature to the right fossil?

Iguanodon

Allosaurus

Gallimimus

Triceratops

Lambeosaurus

Sauroposeidon

Dinosaur Evolution

Fossils have shown that, throughout the eras, different species of dinosaurs shared simila[r] types of bones. Use your stickers to complete the chart below.

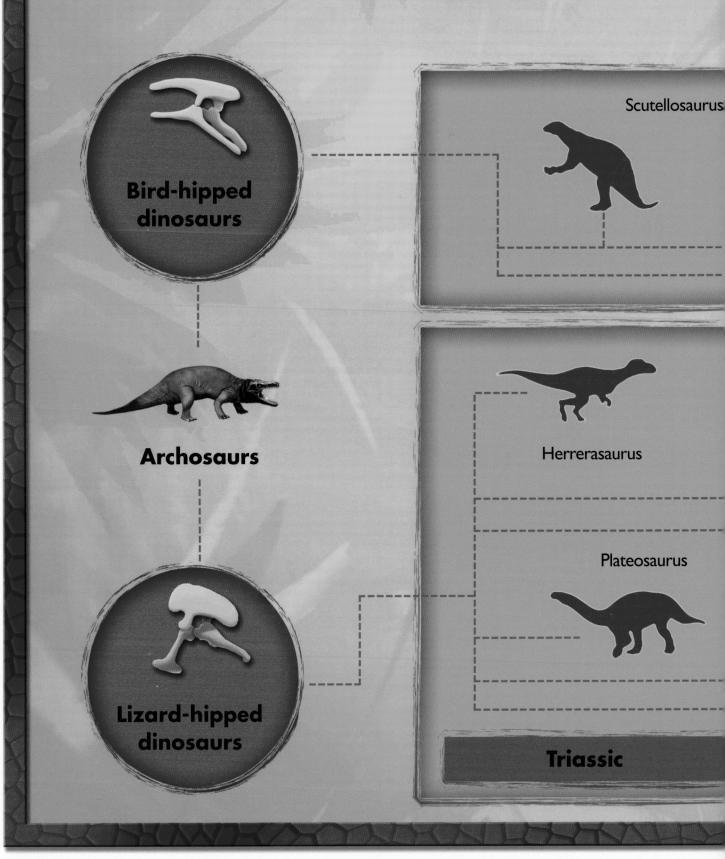

Bird-hipped dinosaurs

Archosaurs

Lizard-hipped dinosaurs

Scutellosaurus

Herrerasaurus

Plateosaurus

Triassic

14

Stegosaurus

Triceratops

Hadrosaurus

Ankylosaurus

Allosaurus

Tyrannosaurus rex

Velociraptor

Diplodocus

Brachiosaurus

Jurassic

Cretaceous

Can You Spot?

Fossils have been found all over the world. Place your stickers over the shadows to uncover a few more special finds!

Amber

Footprints

Skull

Skeleton

Tools